JOY
Is a
CHOICE
You Can
Make
TODAY

JOY

Is a

CHOICE

You Can

Make

TODAY

Kay Warren

R
Revell

a division of Baker Publishing Group
Grand Rapids, Michigan

Published by Revell
a division of Baker Publishing Group
P.O. Box 6287, Grand Rapids, MI 49516-6287
www.revellbooks.com

Printed in the United States of America

ISBN 978-0-8007-2686-7

This book is excerpted from *Choose Joy: Because Happiness Isn't Enough*, published in 2012.

Unless otherwise indicated, Scripture quotations are from the Holy Bible, New International Version®. NIV®. Copyright © 1973, 1978, 1984, 2011 by Biblica, Inc.™ Used by permission of Zondervan. All rights reserved worldwide. www.zondervan.com

Scripture quotations labeled CEV are from the Contemporary English Version © 1991, 1992, 1995 by American Bible Society. Used by permission.

Scripture quotations labeled GW are from *GOD'S WORD*®. © 1995 God's Word to the Nations. Used by permission of Baker Publishing Group.

Scripture quotations labeled MSG are from *The Message* by Eugene H. Peterson, copyright © 1993, 1994, 1995, 2000, 2001, 2002. Used by permission of NavPress Publishing Group. All rights reserved.

Scripture quotations labeled NCV are from the New Century Version®. Copyright © 1987, 1988, 1991 by Word Publishing, a division of Thomas Nelson, Inc. Used by permission. All rights reserved.

Scripture quotations labeled NJB are from THE NEW JERUSALEM BIBLE, copyright © 1985 by Darton, Longman & Todd, Ltd. and Doubleday, a division of Random House, Inc. Reprinted by permission.

Scripture quotations labeled NKJV are from the New King James Version. Copyright © 1982 by Thomas Nelson, Inc. Used by permission. All rights reserved.

Scripture quotations labeled NLT are from the *Holy Bible*, New Living Translation, copyright © 1996, 2004, 2007 by Tyndale House Foundation. Used by permission of Tyndale House Publishers, Inc., Carol Stream, Illinois 60188. All rights reserved.

Scripture quotations labeled Phillips are from The New Testament in Modern English, revised edition—J. B. Phillips, translator. © J. B. Phillips 1958, 1960, 1972. Used by permission of Macmillan Publishing Co., Inc.

16 17 18 19 20 21 22   7 6 5 4 3 2 1

CONTENTS

1

SEEKING A LIFE OF JOY

He will yet fill your mouth with
   laughter
and your lips with shouts of joy.

Job 8:21

Joy does not come easily to me; I'm definitely more of a glass-half-empty kind of gal. In fact, I've struggled with low-level depression as far back as I can remember. As a little girl, I was emotionally intense—I cried easily, agonized over the pain others felt, and carried the weight of the world on my small shoulders. So I'm not talking to you about joy from the perspective of one of those deliriously happy, peppy people who never have a down day. Some days I'm thrilled just to survive!

The Bible gives some commands that are extremely hard to understand and even harder to live out. One of the most difficult commands is to forgive our enemies. In light of the terrible cruelty and evil we can inflict on each other, this seems like asking an armchair athlete to climb Mt. Everest—impossible. The Bible also says not to worry about anything. Anything? Really? Many of us spend a good portion of every waking hour worried or anxious about something. How could God reasonably expect us not to worry? But to me, even harder than either of those two commands is the one found in James 1:2: "When troubles of any kind come your way, consider it an opportunity for great joy" (NLT).

Are you kidding me? When trouble comes my way, my first thoughts aren't usually about experiencing great joy. My typical reaction is more along the lines of fear, panic, worry, and even hopelessness. At the very least, I reserve the right to gripe and moan about my troubles. Hardly an opportunity for great joy.

It's really because of my own struggles to live with joy that I began to explore why my experiences didn't match up with Scripture. I studied the life of Jesus Christ and observed the way biblical characters such as King David; Mary, the mother of Jesus; the apostle

Paul; and James, the half-brother of Jesus, reacted to trouble and sorrow and hard times. For instance, the apostle Paul wrote in Romans 5: رومیه ٥

> We continue to shout our praise even when we're hemmed in with troubles, because we know how troubles can develop passionate patience in us, and how that patience in turn forges the tempered steel of virtue, keeping us alert for whatever God will do next. In alert expectancy such as this, we're never left feeling shortchanged. Quite the contrary—we can't round up enough containers to hold everything God generously pours into our lives through the Holy Spirit! (vv. 3–5 MSG)

I saw a Grand Canyon–sized gap between their lives and mine, and it began to bother me. It was clear that joy—even in pain—was something the biblical writers expected Christians to experience on a regular basis, but I wasn't. Wondering what was different about their faith that allowed them to respond to their circumstances with joy launched me on an intensely personal search. Why was there a discrepancy between my experiences and theirs? I needed to know how to bridge the gigantic gap that was keeping me from living a joyful life.

I'll fill you in on what I'm learning as we go along, but let me jump to the conclusion of the search and tell you the bottom line: *Joy is a choice*. Nothing else

I will say is more critical to the way you live out your years than that small sentence. Joy is a choice. The level of joy you experience is completely and totally up to you. It is not dependent on anyone else—what they do or don't do, how they behave or don't behave. Joy cannot be manipulated by the actions of puny human beings. It is not dependent on the amount of sadness or suffering or difficulties you endure. Joy cannot be held hostage to fear, pain, anger, disappointment, sadness, or grief. At the end of any given day, the amount of joy you experienced is the exact amount of joy you chose to experience. You, my friend, are in charge. The sooner you embrace this pivotal reality, the sooner you can begin to live a more joyful life.

The Bell Curve of Joy

Each of us approaches the idea of joy differently. You may remember from a high school or college astronomy class the Gaussian probability distribution—yeah, probably not—but in simple English, think of a bell curve. At one end of the bell curve are people who don't struggle much to have joy. Their natural temperament is optimistic and upbeat—the glass is half full. Sometimes this type of person really annoys me because she never stops smiling and she seems to float through life with a cheerful, carefree, lighthearted attitude. I mutter to myself, *I wonder if she'd be smiling so big if she had my problems*. Maybe she really is living a charmed life; circumstances haven't slapped her around a whole lot yet. But another possibility is that life *has* slapped her around and she has done some serious spiritual work and learned how to access joy every day. Regardless, some of us are on the positive end of the bell curve.

The majority of us are in the middle of the bell curve. We're moderately happy, not too high and not too low. We don't normally get overly discouraged or depressed. We admit to feeling tired a lot, perhaps a bit bored by the routine, and sometimes even flat. Daily *joy*? I'm not so sure. But, we hastily add, nothing is really *wrong*.

As the bell curve moves downward, there is a smaller group of people at the other end. They are hiding—or not hiding—a cavernous well of depression. Getting out of bed every morning is a chore, and the pleasures of life are gone; smiling and laughing are hard to do. Joy has simply evaporated. That might be because of stress in a relationship, a job change, physical illness, or even deep grief or loss. While those with mild depression can bounce back fairly quickly, those traveling the hard road of profound loss often need years to process their grief before they find their emotional and spiritual equilibrium restored. But the accompanying depression can leave them feeling guilty because they know they're "supposed" to be joyful and they're not.

We don't talk about this much, but many Christians battle depression because of a biochemical imbalance. Some have bipolar disorder, characterized by dramatic mood swings between periods of wild euphoria and disabling depression. Schizophrenia, personality disorders, and many other forms of mental illness—some mild, some severe—plague Christian families just as often as non-Christian families. Physical disability is obvious to the casual observer, but mental brokenness can hide beneath a "normal" exterior. My friend Shannon Royce calls this a "hidden disability."[1] Unfortunately, because of our innate desire to deny our problems and the hard-line stance of those who believe any psychological disruption is mostly a matter of poor discipleship, Christians are often reluctant to talk about mental health issues. This leaves millions suffering alone, ashamed, and, worst of all, unsupported by the church. The stigma is real, and it hurts.

As this curve continues, there's an even smaller group of people at the far end who are contemplating suicide. For some of you, you've given life your best shot, and it's just not enough anymore. You're worn out from the struggle to survive another day, and escaping your painful circumstances has begun to dominate your thoughts. You may even wonder if your family would be better off without you. You've certainly thought that *you* would be better off without experiencing such pain. Joy is so far off in the distance that you believe you will never reach it again, nor are you sure you have the energy to try. You find your struggle extremely difficult to talk about, especially if you're a Christ follower; if mentioning mental illness at church is a risky topic, then talking about suicide or suicidal thoughts can be the ultimate taboo in church.

It's possible you're reading this booklet because someone who cares very much for you is aware of the enormous battle you're fighting and longs for you to experience joy once more. As John Eldredge says, "The story of your life is the story of a long and brutal assault on your heart by the one who knows what you could be and fears it."[2] The enemy of your heart, Satan, does not want you to leave the place of despair, but the lover of your wounded heart, Jesus Christ, has a better plan for you, and it includes joy.

Wherever you are on the bell curve, God has a tender word of encouragement for you: There is concrete, genuine hope for joy in your life. Even if you are in the middle of despair right now, you can experience joy. It is not out of your reach! Happiness in and of itself will never be enough; it's simply too flimsy, too unreliable, too unpredictable. You were meant for something more. You were meant to experience a life of joy.

Created for Joy

I love a book Lewis Smedes wrote many years ago called *How Can It Be All Right When Everything Is All Wrong?* Smedes writes, "You and I were created for joy, and if we miss it, we miss the reason for our existence! Moreover, the reason Jesus Christ lived and died on earth was to restore us to the joy we have lost. . . . His Spirit comes to us with the power to believe that joy is our birthright because the Lord has made this day for us."[3] Jesus died to *restore the joy* that is our inheritance, the joy we lost when Adam and Eve rebelled against God and set the stage for our personal spiritual rebellion.

The good news is that when we realize we've been living in spiritual rebellion against God—not necessarily through gross, terrible actions but by an attitude of "I don't need you, God"—we have the opportunity to receive Jesus Christ as our Savior and Lord. And along with Jesus Christ, we receive his Holy Spirit (Gal. 4:4–7). And with the Holy Spirit comes this beautiful gift of joy, our birthright—not simply one option out of many but our *birthright* (see Gal. 5:22).

God *created* us to be joyful. There's really no doubt about it. But God has left the decision whether to access that joy up to us. You and I get to decide if we're going to choose joy—created by God, bought and paid for by Jesus's death, given as a personal gift from the Holy Spirit—or not.

When you think about it like that, it's hard to imagine why any of us would ever refuse God's gift of joy. But sometimes we do.

Parallel Train Tracks

I used to think that life came in waves. There was a wave of good and pleasant circumstances followed by a wave of bad and unpleasant circumstances, with a lot of ebb and flow in between. Or life was a series of hills and valleys; sometimes we're up, sometimes we're down. But I've come to realize that life is much more like a set of parallel train tracks, with joy and sorrow running simultaneously throughout our days.

Every day of your life good things happen. Beauty, pleasure, fulfillment, and perhaps even excitement occur. That's the track of joy. But every day of your life also holds disappointment, challenges, struggles, and perhaps even losses for you or those you love. That's the track of sorrow. Most of us try to "out-smart" the sorrow track by concentrating our efforts on the joy track, as if by our positive outlook or out-right denial of reality we can make the sorrow track go away. That's impossible, because joy and sorrow will always be linked. And in the strange paradox of the universe, at the exact moment you and I are experiencing pain, we are also aware of the sweetness of loving and the beauty still to be found. Likewise, at the exact moment we are full of delirious delight, we have the nagging realization that things still aren't quite perfect. No matter how "positive" we think or how hard we try to visualize only happiness, the sorrow track remains. One of our toughest challenges in life is to learn how to live on both of those tracks at the same time.

But there's hope! Look ahead with me.

My young grandsons are train fanatics, so I often take them to a quaint outdoor train station where Amtrak stops many times a day. When the ticket agent isn't looking and the coast is completely clear, we stand on the train tracks together and look ahead as far as we can see, hoping to catch the very first sign of an approaching train. As we stand on the tracks and stare into the distant, bright horizon, those parallel tracks become one, no longer distinguishable as two separate tracks.

That's the way it will be for us too. During our lifetime, we "stand on the tracks" looking for signs of Jesus Christ's return. We watch for the sights and sounds that will alert us that his appearance is very close. We stare into the horizon, hoping to catch a glimpse of him. One day, in the brightness of his coming, we will meet him face-to-face. And when we do, the tracks of joy and sorrow will merge. The sorrow will disappear forever, and only the joy will remain. And everything will finally make complete sense. But until that day comes, we live with the parallel tracks of joy . . . and sorrow.

The Definition of Joy

Why are we so reluctant to believe that joy can be a reality for us? I can think of several possible reasons.

The first is that most of us don't have joy models. We don't know many people who have bridged the gap between their experience and what Scripture teaches. Most people we look at are swimming, just like us, in deep waters of very little joy.

Do you think you can name two people who live a life of joy the way the Bible talks about it? Some of you will instantly raise your hands and say, "Absolutely! I know tons of people who are joyful!" I don't mean people who are merely natural extroverts and smile and laugh a lot. I mean men and women who embody the James 1 kind of response to troubles: those who consider it an opportunity for great joy.

That might change the number of joyful people you think you know. So let's keep going. Can you think of five people? How about ten? I doubt that many of you can honestly name ten people who live a joyful life. A few years ago I tried to come up with a list of people who embody what it means to live with joy. I finally thought of two people; one of them was dead, and the other one wasn't me! Without role models to follow, we face a daunting task to figure out what it means to live with joy.

Another reason we're hesitant to believe that joy is within our reach is because we examine our own lives and see how far off we are from the "consider it great joy" response. We say to ourselves, *One of these days I'll go after joy, but not today. I mean, if it falls into my lap, that's great. But I'd be happy just to get through today. Really, I'd be thrilled just to get a good night's sleep! Joy is too big a stretch for me right now.*

So based on the facts that we don't see joy modeled for us and that our own life experience doesn't match what we read in the Bible, many of us have concluded that joy is not going to happen for us. If it does, it will be a total surprise. It will not be anything we can control.

That's why our definition of joy is crucial. If our definition is inadequate, we can wrongly assume that joy and happiness are synonymous and that having happy feelings must mean we are joyful—or that the lack of happy feelings must mean we don't have joy. We spend the day at an amusement park or a sporting event or have a fantastic vacation and conclude that the happy feelings we're experiencing equal joy. Or we observe someone who always seems upbeat and optimistic and think they have joy.

Not necessarily. You can't see into their hearts. You can't see into their lives to know how they respond when tough times come. You're looking at the face they present to the world, and you're concluding that's what joy is.

But if joy is not warm, fuzzy feelings or a smiling face, and it is not dependent on circumstances, what is it?

A few years ago I read a quote by Paul Sailhamer, who said that joy comes from knowing God is in control of our lives.[4] I liked that a lot, but I wanted more words around it to adequately express what I believe Scripture teaches about how to live a joyful life. I've written a definition of joy and memorized it so I can remind myself of the powerful truths when I'm feeling shaky: Joy is the settled assurance that God is in control of all the details of my life, the quiet confidence that ultimately everything is going to be all right, and the determined choice to praise God in all things.

Did you catch that? Joy is a settled conviction *about* God. It's a quiet confidence *in* God. And joy is a determined choice to give my praise *to* God.

My prayer is that you will memorize this definition and that it will come to your mind when your world seems to be falling apart. I know how profoundly my life is changing as I develop a settled conviction *about* God and his goodness. My confidence *in* God is growing as I trust that he is working behind the scenes to fit all the details of my life into his good plan. And my determination to give my praise *to* God is slowly leading me to the joy I've always longed for. I want the same for you!

When I say, "Everything will be all right," it's not the equivalent of saying "Don't worry, be happy" or some other nifty little phrase. Believing that ultimately everything is going to be all right takes into account car accidents, cancer, bankruptcy, miscarriage, depression, and every other grief we face. Choosing to believe that God is always working, knitting together the fragments of our lives, always in control of it all, means that life *will* work together for our good and his glory.

Of course, we want all the answers now, today, this moment. And we want more than simple answers. We want explanations in triplicate with a certification that God is qualified to make those decisions, thank you very much. That's why the word *ultimately* is in our definition of joy. God doesn't promise answers or explanations on demand. He promises joy.

So joy is much more than external things. It's much more than that happy, giddy feeling that may come every once in a while. The joy that God speaks of in his Word is something you can count on. It has nothing to do with the circumstances of our lives—and that, I've discovered, is very good news.

In the chapters to come, we will look at how we know God created us for joy and how Jesus's life of joy and sorrow gives us permission to choose joy even in the midst of pain. Joy is not just a nice add-on to the Christian life, the bow on top of the package. It is God's *purpose* for your life. It's time to embrace it!

2

SHOWING
OUR TRUE COLORS

Our mouths were filled with laughter,
 our tongues with songs of joy.
Then it was said among the nations,
 "The LORD has done great things
 for them."

Psalm 126:2

James, the half-brother of Jesus, who wrote the
Epistle of James, did not accept that Jesus was the
Messiah during Jesus's lifetime, but later he became
a pastor and a pillar of the early church. Tradition
tells us that he was martyred for his faith, so I'm eager

to listen to what this man, who penned the famous words that are the basis for this booklet, has to say. He is certainly someone who put his money where his mouth was. He wrote in James 1:2–4:

> Consider it a sheer gift, friends, when tests and challenges come at you from all sides. You know that under pressure, your faith-life is forced into the open and shows its true colors. So don't try to get out of anything prematurely. Let it do its work so you become mature and well-developed, not deficient in any way. (MSG)

James says that in tough times, our "faith-life is forced into the open and shows its true colors." That's a rather daunting thought: No matter what you *say* you believe or what others *think* you believe, there's no hiding or pretending when the bottom falls out— when you receive a dreaded diagnosis, a loved one dies, your finances collapse, your kids decide to make a mess out of their lives, someone goes to prison, or mental illness destroys a relationship.

The faith-life I claim to have is revealed in those moments—not to God, because he already knows the true state of my heart, but to me. My true colors can no longer be hidden beneath the Sunday smiles or the polite exchanges with a neighbor at the mailbox. Suddenly, what lurked below the waterline of my soul is uncovered, and all my great statements of faith are worthless. What matters in those times is what I *do*.

Sometimes our reaction to a difficult situation is so far from a biblical response that we step back in shock and think, *I thought I was a better Christian than that. I thought I was a more mature believer. I thought I had more oomph in my faith. I've got nothing!* As painful as it is to become aware of the holes in our faith, we can be grateful that tough times give us an accurate report of where we need to change and grow.

But there is another unexpected benefit that comes when my faith-life is brought out into the open through painful circumstances: A watching world gets to see what believing in God really means. In Philippians 2:14–15, the apostle Paul says, "Do everything readily and cheerfully—no bickering, no second-guessing allowed! Go out into the world uncorrupted, a breath of fresh air in this squalid and polluted society. Provide people with a glimpse of good living and of the living God. Carry the light-giving Message into the night" (MSG). Another translation says, "among whom you shine like stars in the dark world" (NCV).

When the sky falls in and we are thrown into chaos, our faith-life is suddenly on display for everyone—neighbors, friends, unbelieving family, and co-workers—to see. And the Bible says our faith-life should provide a stark contrast to the life of unbelievers, so much so that it would be like looking at a brilliant star against the inky blackness of a dark night sky—you can't help but notice the difference.

Many friends and acquaintances may look at you with avid curiosity: *How does a Christian respond in this situation? What does a person who goes to church every week and has one of those fish stickers on the back of her car do when bad stuff happens?* Often they are really asking the questions not to judge you or to criticize you but because they genuinely want to know if being a Christian makes a practical difference in your life. When you react exactly the same way they would in a crisis, they can't help but wonder, *Why in the world would I need her God?* We have to ask ourselves the same hard question: If being a Christian makes no difference in the way we respond to problems, what good is our faith? What have we gained by going to church every weekend, attending Bible studies, memorizing Scripture, and sending our kids to a Christian school if, when trouble comes, we're just like everyone else?

This takes us back to our image of the parallel train tracks of sorrow and joy. When trials expose our faith-life, will others see us embracing both the joy and the pain? Those around us need to recognize that both of these elements are part of life, and both give us hope for heaven.

Building a Stronger Faith

As I've already told you, I struggle to choose joy as my initial response to bad news. My first reaction is usually worry or anxiety, not joy, not thanking God for this "gift." And when I see that kind of reaction in myself, I am disappointed to realize how far I still have to go to be a mature woman of God.

But that's exactly the point James is making. The only way to grow up spiritually—to become mature and well-developed in our faith—is to go through the fire of testing, trials, and troubles. An untested faith is an unreliable faith. We hate the process of refining that makes us like Jesus Christ in our character because it involves pain and sorrow and stress and upheaval. Ronald Dunn says, "Why is the struggle so relentless? Because God wants to change us, and we don't want to be changed."[1] All of us want the *product* of trials and pain—maturity—without having to go through the *process.* But James warns us not to try to wriggle out of the hard times too soon; if we do, we will short-circuit the process and remain immature. I don't want to be a spiritual or emotional infant. Do you?

Time for another true confession. I'll admit I've told God, *I'm okay with staying a spiritual baby; I can live with remaining immature and underdeveloped because growing hurts!* But in my heart of hearts, that's

27

not what I want. I want my faith-life to be sturdy and strong, mature and well-developed. I'm willing to let trials and troubles expose my faith-life so that I'll know to stay on the path until I'm finished, not just for my own benefit but for those who are watching my life.

A watching world of friends, family, neighbors, co-workers, and casual acquaintances has questions about spiritual matters, especially as they relate to suffering and the presence of evil in the world and in their own lives. They are misinformed and confused about God, Jesus, the Holy Spirit, and the Bible. How we respond to trials—hopefully, like a star shining brightly in a dark sky—can earn us the opportunity to speak to their questions and accurately reflect to them who God really is.

Acts 16:16–34 gives an account of Paul and Silas imprisoned unjustly in Philippi for healing a demon-possessed young girl. After they were arrested, they were severely beaten and thrown into an inner cell where their feet were locked in stocks. The Bible says that around midnight Paul and Silas were praying and singing hymns to God and "the other prisoners were listening to them" (v. 25) when a severe earthquake shook the foundations of the prison, causing the prisoners to be freed from their chains.

It was customary for a jailer to commit suicide if his prisoners escaped, knowing the authorities would kill him anyway for his failure to secure those left in his care. That night, when the jailer was preparing to stab himself with his sword in response to the open prison doors, Paul shouted that they were all still in their cells. The Bible records the jailer's astonishment; he trembled and fell before Paul and Silas, asking, "Sirs, what must I do to be saved?"

Then Paul and Silas—having earned the right to testify to who God is by their response to an unjust beating and imprisonment—told this jailer how he and his family could be saved. The jailer and his household followed Jesus Christ and were baptized. The account ends with this verse: "The jailer brought them into his house and set a meal before them; he was filled with joy because he had come to believe in God—he and his whole household" (v. 34).

I'm not convinced that I would have responded the way Paul and Silas did. I wish I could confidently say that I would have been praying and singing hymns at the top of my lungs, but I think I might have been weeping and wailing at the top of my lungs—letting everyone know that an injustice had been done and that somebody had better make it right quickly!

But not Paul and Silas. Their faith-lives were exposed for a watching world of felons and jailers to observe, and their true colors were revealed. They shone brilliantly like stars in the black-velvet night sky of their prison chains, and in so doing, they made God look really good—so good that a hardened jailer, used to the phony-baloney protests of innocence from criminals, knew something was *very* different about these men . . . and their God. He wanted what they had, and he wanted it for his family as well. Their settled assurance about God, their quiet confidence that ultimately everything would be all right, and their determined choice to praise God in all things opened the door of salvation for the jailer and his loved ones.

What did the jailer gain from his encounter with Paul and Silas? Not only salvation but joy!

The Watching World

What do you think the answer would be if you asked your friends, "Does God smile? Does he smile at you?" Many people—even Christians, if we would admit it—believe that God is a grumpy old man having a bad eternity (day) sitting up in heaven watching with his eagle eyes for ways to squish the tiniest bits of happiness we might find. *Smile? Probably not. Smile at me? Not if he knows what I'm really like.*

The world has a skewed view of Jesus as well. Was there ever a more maligned, misunderstood, and misrepresented figure in history than Jesus Christ? He is alternatively revered as the Savior of the world, the restorer of broken hearts, minds, and relationships, and reviled as the single most disruptive person ever to live, blamed for global wars, nationalistic opportunism, and interpersonal conflict.

When it comes to the Holy Spirit, there's total confusion among non-Christians. Who or what is a "Holy Spirit"? Visions of Casper the Friendly Ghost, or the Haunted Mansion at Disneyland, or the tongue-tied Mr. Bean ("the Holy Spigot") come to mind—it just sounds weird or spooky or goofy.

Most people also believe the Bible is a book of doom and gloom, full of tedious, outdated rules that don't make sense in our ultrasophisticated world of technology and innovation. Or they're afraid to read the Bible, fearing they won't be able to make sense of what they read or assuming they will be bombarded with words of condemnation, shame, and guilt.

A watching world needs to hear from us that God personifies joy. They need to know that Jesus was a man of joy as well as a man of sorrows. They need to know that the Holy Spirit gives us joy as a birthright to claim. They need to know that the Bible is a book of joy, with more references to joy, laughter, and merriment than to tears, sorrow, and sadness. Remember, we have to constantly ask ourselves, *Why would they believe God created joy, or Jesus was a man of joy, or the*

Holy Spirit gives joy, or the Bible is a book of joy if all they have to evaluate is my life? Am I perpetuating the myth that God is a God of sorrow because I can't access the life of joy he intended for me?

In this season of my life, I'm even more aware that my faith-life is on display. For a long time I wanted to live a joyful, passionate life so that my children would have a strong role model as they developed their own faith-lives. But now I have grandchildren . . . I have nieces and nephews . . . I have young women friends who look up to me . . . and it's more important than ever to show them the way to a life of joy—not happiness, but joy. I want my kids to be able to say, "My mom had a lot to deal with, but she overcame her personality. She didn't let her struggles define her. And at the end of the day, my mom was a woman of joy." I want my grandkids to be able to say, "My grammy loved me, and she made me feel special every time I was with her." I want my nieces and nephews to be able to say, "Aunt Kay was a little quirky, but she loved Jesus, and she was a woman of joy." I want the young women I work with to be able to say, "Kay wasn't perfect, but she found her joy in the Lord, even when she had many reasons to be sad." When the people who are watching me most closely make their short list of people who live with joy, I want to be on that list. Don't you want to be on somebody's short list?

Dancing with Shouts of Joy

By the way, in case you're wondering about the answer to the question I posed a few paragraphs back—Does God smile at you?—here's his answer:

> Yahweh your God is there with you, the warrior-Saviour. He will rejoice over you with happy song, he will renew you by his love, he will dance with shouts of joy for you. (Zeph. 3:17 NJB)

He doesn't just smile at you . . . he sings and dances with shouts of joy for you! My friend, he knows all about you. He knows how often you fail to get it right; he knows the times you earnestly desire to shine like a star on a dark night but don't quite make it. He knows the truest intentions of your heart; he sees where you're trying. He's keenly aware of the brutal pain that has ripped you into pieces; his heart aches with yours as you struggle to accept the process that makes you mature. He knows what no one else will ever know. And his response to all he sees within you . . . within me? This makes me weep. *He dances for us with shouts of joy.*

This is the God I want a watching world to know through me.

3

REDISCOVERING JESUS, THE MAN OF JOY

> I have told you this so that my joy may be in you and that your joy may be complete.
>
> John 15:11

I think one of the reasons we forget that the Bible is a book of joy is that we don't see Jesus, the main character in the Bible, as a man of joy. Many of you know Jesus well already. He's been there on your best days, days when your heart was ready to explode with excitement. *This is the top. This is the pinnacle. I am so happy!* And Jesus was with you.

But Jesus has also been with you in the worst of times, times when you thought your heart was going to disintegrate from sorrow, when the pain was so overwhelming that you didn't know how you were going to survive the next minute, let alone the rest of your life. He has been there.

The reason Jesus can comfort us in sorrow is because he, too, suffered. Isaiah 53:3 says, "He was despised and rejected by mankind, a man of suffering, and familiar with pain." It's easy to conclude from this passage that Jesus was *just* a man of sorrows. But if we look at him only through that lens, we're going to sell him short, because Jesus was also a man of joy.

And Jesus Laughed

God created the heavens and the earth, as well as humankind; unfortunately, our first human father and mother rebelled against God, leading to sin and sorrow being unleashed on our planet. As part of a plan far beyond our finite understanding, God the Father gave Jesus the role of becoming the Savior of the world to restore the terminally ruptured relationship between us and God. In that role, Jesus would leave the perfection of heaven and come to earth, where he would know immense suffering and pain

36

and sorrow and heartache and betrayal and loss. He would become a man of sorrows. But in his essence, Jesus was a man of joy.

This is a critical point: In Jesus's *role*, he was a man of sorrows. But in his *essence*—his unchanging nature—he was a man of joy. In fact, the Bible tells us, "The Son of Man came, enjoying life" (Luke 7:34 Phillips). I love that! The Son of Man didn't come bent over in pain. He didn't arrive with a scowl on his face. He wasn't a killjoy who couldn't survive without his box of tissues. He came eating and drinking and loving life—"feasting," as another version says.[1]

So why is it that throughout history, Jesus has been portrayed as sad, serious, somber? Why have we flattened Jesus into a one-dimensional character instead of understanding that he was both a man of sorrows and a man of joy?

Consider the most common images of Jesus, such as the sanitized image of Jesus that hangs in Sunday school classrooms all over America. This was the picture I grew up with in my church, and you may have too. In this image, Jesus's hair is perfectly styled, with soft curls framing his face. There's no sweat or grit or imperfection on his face, not a single enlarged pore on his cheeks. No pimples, no wrinkles, no laugh lines around his mouth; there's not even a hint of a smile on his smooth face. As a kid, I remember thinking I had to be very serious around the Jesus painting; you could laugh anywhere else in the room, but not next to Jesus!

While many evangelical churches display the "gentle Jesus, meek and mild, who wouldn't harm a flea" painting, other churches fill their sacred spaces with images of Jesus in his most agonizing moments. In fact, almost all fine art throughout the centuries portrays him on his most grievous day on earth—the day he was beaten and bloodied, with a crown of thorns viciously thrust into his scalp; the day he collapsed under the weight of the wooden cross he carried on his lacerated back through the streets of Jerusalem; the day he was brutally murdered.

Some of the well-known portrayals of Jesus focus on the aftermath of his crucifixion, when he was taken down from the cross, limp and broken. One of the most emotionally stirring pieces of art is Michelangelo's *Pietà*, with the lifeless body of Jesus draped across his mother's lap. Every woman who has ever birthed a child resonates with the pathos of his mother's desire to gather the dead child of her womb close to her heart one more time.

I know why fine art has captured Jesus in his most painful moments—there's no mystery here. It's why he came to earth; Jesus came to die. He came to be our Savior, and being our Savior meant pain. Hurt. Sorrow. Suffering. To record that in art is perfectly appropriate; it really happened, and it was even worse than it appears.

The problem is that we don't balance those graphic images of Jesus with other lighthearted images, and we are left to conclude that his was a life of sorrow that ended in tragedy. In my efforts to learn how to choose joy—even in this imperfect world—I set out to discover images of Jesus that show him in the lighter moments that reflect his essence, not just his role.

The first one I found is probably the most famous. It's called *The Laughing Christ*. You won't believe where it was first seen: the January 1970 issue of *Playboy*. (I do not expect you to go find that issue to verify that I'm telling you the truth. Just believe me.) Hugh Hefner was captivated by the idea that Jesus could laugh. It was so startling to him, so against what he had seen all his life, that he published it.

Another joyful picture is called *The Laughing Jesus*. I tried to find it at a Christian bookstore a few years ago, and they told me they didn't carry it. It was a special order, and I'd have to wait three weeks. I thought, *What's going on here? I can get more art than I can shake a stick at of Jesus suffering, wounded, bleeding, dying. But I can't find a single picture to put in my house that shows him laughing and enjoying life?*

Jesus was a vibrant, compassionate man, a man of both sorrow and joy who could enter fully into life with all its brokenness. That sounds like someone I'd like to get to know. If he was a man of sorrows *and* could experience joy, maybe I can too.

So I want to shake up the perceptions of Jesus that you've been taught your entire life. I'll let Jesus prove it to you himself through his attitude, his words, and his actions. We've been talking about the lack of joy role models—there is none better than Jesus Christ. His life is a model for any of us who are seeking a life of joy.

A Man of Joy through His Attitude

Three of the Gospels record an incident when parents crowded near to Jesus, holding out their infants and children for him to touch (Matt. 19:13–15; Mark 10:13–16; Luke 18). Scripture says that he "took the children in his arms, placed his hands on them and blessed them" (Mark 10:16). While parents today are especially cautious about strangers being around their children, parents have always been wary of exposing their children to danger. The parents who were so eager to have Jesus touch and hold and bless their children must have sensed that he had a tender heart toward their little ones.

Even if the parents were confident in Jesus's ability to charm the kids, that doesn't mean that the children would automatically be comfortable around him, but there's no record of them shrinking away from his touch. We all know that kids have a way of sensing who the fun people are and who they don't really want to be around. My grandkids are the joy of my heart and we love being together, but I suspect my grandkids love their papa in a special way. The other day, four-year-old Caleb whispered in Rick's ear, "Papa, you're my favorite friend." They love to be around Rick because he is the funmeister! He's loud and boisterous; he loves to tickle and play and laugh and do crazy things that bring them great delight.

Recently, at Grandparents' Day at our grandkids' elementary school, we visited Kaylie's and Cassidy's classrooms and then walked with them out to the playground for recess. I, ever the obedient rule follower, sat down with the other rule-following grandparents under the awning in the outdoor lunch area. Rick ran past me with our eight-year-old granddaughter, Kaylie, and six-year-old Cassidy in tow. Over his shoulder he shouted, "I'm gonna go play with the girls on the playground!" Of course, that made me nervous. *Should he be doing that? Is that against the school rules?* Within seconds, a small crowd of grade schoolers, drawn by shouts of laughter and delight, had gathered around Rick as he played a raucous game of "Red Light, Green Light" with our granddaughters. Soon, dozens of screaming boys and girls were running toward Rick when he said,

"Green light," and then shrieking with mock terror as he chased them back to their safe zone during the "red light" portion of the game. Over all the ear-splitting laughter and noise, I could hear Kaylie's exuberant declaration, "My papa always starts a party!" So true.

Kids *know*! They know when someone is fun. After Jesus gathered the children in his arms, hugged and kissed them as only God-in-flesh could do, I can only imagine the giggle fests the children had. I wonder if sometimes he would draw a child to him and whisper in her ear, "See that tree over there? I made that tree! Isn't it the coolest tree you've ever seen?" He interacted with them in such a way that they wanted to be around him. That tells us a lot about who he was.

Not only did children love Jesus, but crowds of adults followed him everywhere, so much so that it became difficult for him to get away for private prayer.

The fact that people were around Jesus all the time doesn't mean he was a drop-dead-gorgeous hunk. In fact, the Bible tells us, "He wasn't some handsome king. Nothing about the way he looked made him attractive to us" (Isa. 53:2 CEV). Something indefinably charismatic about Jesus drew people to him; something about his demeanor and the way he interacted with people was attractive. He was someone others wanted to be around.

It's no wonder, then, that Jesus was invited to *a lot* of parties. You and I don't invite dull, boring people to parties unless we feel some sort of obligation. We try to invite people who are interesting and fun and who will add some spice and sparkle.

So it's interesting to me that not only did Jesus get invited to a lot of parties, but many of his stories are based around parties. Most of them had to do with who got invited to parties and who didn't. That makes sense when we remember that Jesus enjoyed life. He was so fully engaged in these parties that some people accused him of being a glutton or a drunk.

Jesus wasn't a drunk. He was just a party guy, someone who was out there mingling with people, not sitting in a corner by a potted palm tree. And people loved it. Jesus's attitude toward life showed that he was a man of joy.

A Man of Joy through His Words

Part of rediscovering Jesus, the man of joy, involves taking a look at how he conveyed his joyful essence through his words. We don't usually think of Jesus as having a comedy act. But he told jokes! He was, in fact, hilariously funny. The very idea that Jesus told jokes and went for the punch lines with his audience might be shocking to some of you who are used to thinking of him only as the somber and serious guy. The problem is that you and I just don't get his humor. The chasm of language, culture, and time keeps us from fully understanding Jesus's intent. Since we don't get his humor, we tend to skip right over it.

Take Luke 18:25, for example. If I asked you to read it out loud, you would probably read it in a flat, monotone voice with no particular emphasis or much of an inflection: "For it is easier for a camel to go through the eye of a needle than for a rich man to enter the kingdom of God" (NKJV). Boring! But that's the way we typically read Scripture—like we're reading the phone book! I guarantee that Jesus didn't say it like that. He was using an exaggerated word picture, a common way in Jewish culture to say something funny. His audience loved it—they thought he was a riot! They couldn't believe the funny lines that fell from his lips and the jokes he was telling.

Why did he use so much humor? The great thing about humor that's still true today is that once you get people laughing, you can slide the truth in there too. You don't resist truth as much if you're laughing. So Jesus used humor to make his point, to tell truths to those who were listening who might be cautious about accepting his teaching.

I want to show you a couple other punch lines in Jesus's teachings.

In Matthew 23:24, Jesus warns scribes and Pharisees, "Blind guides! You strain your water so you won't accidentally swallow a gnat, but you swallow a camel!" (NLT). Jesus was referring to their habit of concentrating on teeny-tiny laws concerning washing their hands and ignoring the great big laws of loving their neighbor. That's like straining out a tiny bug that you're choking on while you swallow a camel whole, according to Jesus. To us, it's not that funny; to his audience, it was great, edgy humor.

But my favorite joke from Jesus is in Matthew 7:3, 5. Jesus is talking to one of the large crowds that gathered around him on a regular basis. Evidently, he had noticed his disciples' petty arguments, because Jesus again turns to exaggeration and metaphor to say, "And why worry about a speck in your friend's eye when you have a log in your own? . . . First get rid of the log in your own eye; then you will see well enough to deal with the speck in your friend's eye" (NLT).

Try it yourself—try reading these verses to your best friend or your small group when you're together this week. Get loud! Use your hands to exaggerate the tiny speck that is in your friend's eye, and then use *big* hand motions to indicate the gigantic log that is in your own eye. I promise that you and your friends will be smiling, at the very least, if not laughing by the time you're through with your little experiment. The absurdity of getting all worked up about a small fault your friend has when you have a colossal error in your own life will become clear to you, and you will catch a glimpse of Jesus's powerful communication style. When we read these stories with new eyes, his words come alive. His relationships come alive. He becomes a real man talking to real people. A real man of joy.

A Man of Joy through His Actions

We read in John 2 that Jesus was at a wedding (another party!) in the town of Cana. It was customary to offer wine at a wedding. Now, I don't know if more people than the host was expecting showed up, but toward the end of the celebration, he ran out of wine. All he had left was jugs of water.

Mary, Jesus's mother, was there. She looked at Jesus and said, more or less, "You fix this. You can figure something out."

Jesus answered, "Why did you come to me? My time has not yet come" (John 2:4 GW).

Through the years, when I've heard this story told at church, I've imagined Jesus saying, "Mom! Would you back off? You're blowing my cover! Please just chill out and leave me alone." Jesus is harsh with her, puts her down, and tells her to mind her own business.

But now I don't believe he talked that way to her. Now that I understand Jesus more fully, I think his words sounded more like this, said in a friendly, con-spiratorial whisper: "Shhhh! Mom! Thank you for believing in me. I really appreciate it. But today's not the day. It's not time yet, Mom."

The interesting thing to me is that Jesus went ahead and turned the water into wine—and not just a cheap grocery store wine but an incredibly fine wine with a rich bouquet. The Bible said it was the best wine served that day.

I don't know exactly why Jesus performed his first miracle at a wedding, but I think it fits perfectly with his joyful essence to choose a festive social event to unveil his public ministry. I think that says something vitally important about him.

Another story that reflects Jesus as a man of joy is in Matthew 14. Jesus has been ministering to thou-sands of people for hours, and he can't escape the crowds. Greatly in need of some peace and quiet, he tells his disciples to get in a boat and go to the other side of the lake while he goes up on a mountainside to pray.

In the middle of the night, the disciples are startled—scared spitless, actually—to see Jesus gliding across the water to them. The Bible says they screamed in their terror, thinking Jesus was a ghost. Before we put them down for their fear, it's good to remember that no one had ever seen someone walk on water before.

Jesus tries to calm them down by identifying himself and urges them to not be afraid. Evidently, Peter is quick to accept that the water-walking apparition is Jesus because he calls out, "Jesus? Is that really you? If so, tell me to come to you on the water."

Jesus says, "It's me, Peter. Come on down!"

Peter hops out of the boat and starts walking on the water toward Jesus. Jesus is smiling at him, expecting him to come.

All of a sudden, Peter's focus is broken as a chilly breeze off the lake pulls at his long robes and the precarious nature of his adventure hits him like a ton of bricks. *I'm walking on water!* He looks down, and the minute he looks down, he starts to sink. "Lord, save me!" he screams. Matthew 14:31 says, "Immediately Jesus reached out his hand and caught him. 'You of little faith,' he said, 'why did you doubt?'"

My entire life I've heard that verse read in a tone of voice that conveys condemnation: "Peter! How many times have I told you I would take care of you? Give me your hand—right now. Get up here, you of little faith."

I don't believe that anymore. God does not criticize us or put us down when we take baby steps of faith. Peter *was* taking steps of faith when he got out of the boat. God knew he needed encouragement, not disapproval.

I believe that Jesus looked at Peter with tenderness in his eyes, pulled Peter close to him, and said,

"Peter, Peter! Oh, you of little faith. Why did you doubt me? I told you I'd take care of you. I'm here for you." That's the way God reacts to us when we mess up in our attempts to serve him.

In another story in Matthew 14, the Bible says that five thousand people heard that Jesus was in town and came to him seeking healing for their sick. The number in the crowd was probably closer to fifteen thousand because you have to figure the men brought their wives, who brought their children.

As it got close to evening, the disciples began to be concerned about feeding the mass of people who didn't seem to be in a hurry to go home. They strategized among themselves and figured the best plan was for Jesus to tell the crowd to disperse and go find food on their own. They had their speech all memorized and thought Jesus would applaud their organizational skills. However, Jesus threw them a huge curveball when he responded to their plan with these words in verse 16: "They do not need to go away. You give them something to eat."

What did he expect them to do? The disciples couldn't feed fifty people, let alone fifteen thousand! But he looked at them and said, "You feed them."

Again, we're so used to glossing over familiar passages of Scripture that we miss the punch of the story, and our dry, listless way of reading it out loud just compounds the problem. Jesus didn't turn to his disciples and say, "You guys blew it again! I put you in charge of the lunch, and what did you do? You didn't even count all the women and the children. I can't ever depend on you to take care of things. I have to do it myself around here."

That wasn't the way it was. He took that moment to show them that while they were inadequate to take care of the need of the moment, they didn't need to worry. He would take care of them, and he did. He took a little boy's lunch of fish and loaves and he broke it and he multiplied it and he fed all those people. And there was so much left over, the Bible says, that the extra food filled twelve baskets. Jesus took care of his followers. He didn't put his disciples down as they were trying to figure out how to do what he asked them to do.

Jesus was a man of joy. *He was a man of joy!* He showed it in his attitude; he drew crowds who couldn't get enough of him. He showed it in his words; he was a master communicator who impacted those who listened to him in person two thousand years ago. He showed joy in his actions; he treated people with good humor and patient understanding of their human foibles, and he was skillful in bringing them to the spiritual realizations they needed.

His joyful essence was evidenced particularly in the way he interacted with his disciples. He spent three years with them, day in and day out. He did not spend those three years with them as a lecturer on the speaking circuit who used them to organize his comings and goings: "Okay, let's go over the agenda. Who will be taking care of the donkey this afternoon? Oh, and make sure the people know that I'm coming." He didn't relate as a distant professor who made them sit still while he instilled knowledge: "Now, I have three points I want to make today, and I'll be testing you later. Is everybody writing down what I'm saying?"

No, Jesus lived his life with them. They saw him when he was sweaty and stinky from a long walk from village to village. They knew when his stomach growled from hunger pains. They probably heard him pass gas and burp a few dozen times. I'm not saying that to be sensational; I really believe it. Jesus spent nearly every waking—and sleeping—hour with these twelve men for three years. How could they not really *know* each other? I'm sure Jesus and his friends shared many private jokes, funny stories, and poignant memories, which happens only when people spend intentional time together. I am convinced they laughed till their sides hurt at every opportunity. He loved them and invested in their lives as individuals. I think he probably knew the names of their family members for a couple of generations back; he knew the beauty and dysfunction that created each one of them. He believed in them, ultimately entrusting them with his gospel message of a joyous relationship with God. As his time on earth drew to a close, they were the ones he wanted near him—these friends who had become brothers.

Joy in a World of Sorrow

Why does it matter that Jesus was a man of joy? It matters so much more than you might have ever realized! Some of you may need permission to seek a life of joy for yourself. The burden of grief that you carry, the health issues, the relational pain, the financial questions, the internal struggles and temptations no one else knows about—sometimes all of that weighs you down so much that you give up on the idea of joy. At times I have felt I could identify with the title given to Jesus in Isaiah; I could call myself "Kay Warren, woman of sorrows." Perhaps that title fits you as well. Many of us need permission to recognize sorrow but go beyond it and still choose a life of joy.

Yes, Jesus suffered, but we can't stop there. We can't let that truth dominate how we act and how we speak about him. There was a *reason* why Jesus chose to endure all that he did. There was a reason why he allowed himself to be bloodied and beaten and tortured. Hebrews 12:2 gives us an insider, behind-the-scenes look at why Jesus allowed all of that to happen: "For the joy set before him, he endured the cross."

But what was the joy that was set before him? What joy was so rich, so satisfying, so deep that he was willing to suffer such terrible abuse? *You* were the joy set before him! *I* was the joy set before him! He suffered so he could be reconciled with *you*. With *me*. When people spat at him, his disciples left him, and everyone mocked him, he was thinking of the joy. When he was flogged, when that cruel crown of thorns was jammed on his head, and when he hung on the cross, he got through it because he was holding on to the joy of presenting us to God. *Here he is, Father; I brought him back to you.* The joy of restoring the broken relationship, of living with me and you forever . . . that was the joy set before him, that was the joy that kept him nailed to the cross.

Jesus knew that for him to fulfill his God-given role here on earth, he would have to experience abandonment, betrayal, torture, and death. Yet knowing full well what was ahead of him, he chose to laugh, to tell jokes, to roll around on the ground with children, to build rich relationships, to have meaningful work, to experience joy.

Jesus's life is an illustration of the two train tracks converging into one. He shows us how to see joy, a joy that sometimes comes in darkness. And for that joy he endured the greatest suffering anyone has known.

This is what Jesus's life tells me: It is possible to experience enormous burdens, pain, and struggles—the weight of the world on our frail shoulders—and still experience joy. Jesus's life reminds me that joy is possible no matter what. His life gives me permission to seek a life of joy for myself even in a world of sorrow.

Right now, today, you can begin to choose joy. Jesus, a full-of-joy kind of Savior, thought of the joy of being reunited with you as he died on the cross. His death provided a way for you to come into relationship with him. When you enter into that relationship, you can have joy even in sorrow. Will you choose joy today?

Now, can I encourage you to make God's good news your own? As I said earlier, when we realize we've been living in spiritual rebellion against God, we have the opportunity to receive Jesus Christ as our Savior and Lord. God loves you, has offered forgiveness and his presence to you. In John 3:36 the Bible says, "Whoever accepts and trusts the Son gets in on everything!" (MSG).

Right now, you can talk to God, a conversation that will change the trajectory of your life. Say to him, "I believe in you. I want to receive you into my life. Thank you, Jesus, for dying on the cross for my sins. Please help me to know you, trust you, and love you every day."

Welcome to the family of God! As you make that prayer a reality and continue to choose joy, I encourage you to find a local church where you can receive the love and acceptance of God through fellow members. And I hope you'll tell me of your decision too— you can connect with me at www.KayWarren.com.

NOTES

Chapter 1 Seeking a Life of Joy

1. Shannon Royce, Chosen Families.org, http://chosenfamilies.org/welcome-to-chosen-families/.

2. John Eldredge, *Waking the Dead* (Nashville: Thomas Nelson, 2003), 34.

3. Lewis Smedes, *How Can It Be All Right When Everything Is All Wrong?*, rev. ed. (Wheaton: Harold Shaw, 1999), 27, 43.

4. Sailhamer's exact quote is, "Joy is that deep settled confidence that God is in control of every area of my life." Cited in Tim Hansel, *You Gotta Keep Dancin'* (Colorado Springs: David C. Cook, 1998), 54.

Chapter 2 Showing Our True Colors

1. Ronald Dunn, *When Heaven Is Silent: Trusting God When Life Hurts* (Fort Washington, PA: CLC Publications, 2008), 27.

Chapter 3 Rediscovering Jesus, the Man of Joy

1. Matthew 11:16–19 MSG.

Kay Warren, cofounder with her husband, Rick, of Saddleback Church in Lake Forest, California, is a Bible teacher, an international speaker, and a best-selling author. Kay is a respected advocate for those living with HIV & AIDS, orphaned and vulnerable children, as well as those affected by mental illness. She founded Saddleback's HIV & AIDS Initiative. Kay is the author of *Choose Joy: Because Happiness Isn't Enough* and *Say Yes to God* and coauthor of *Foundations*, a popular systematic theology course used by churches worldwide. Her children are Amy and Josh, and Matthew who is in heaven, and she has five grandchildren. Learn more at www.kaywarren.com and follow her on Facebook (Kay Warren) and on Twitter (@KayWarren1).

Stay connected with Kay

www.KayWarren.com

Visit www.KayWarren.com to connect with other readers, sign up for the free email devotions, and order the *Choose Joy* curriculum. In addition, you will find information and resources about the passions of Kay's heart: orphans and vulnerable children, a Christian response to HIV and AIDS, the PEACE Plan, and encouragement for pastors' wives, as well as current articles she has written.

KAY WARREN App

Download the free iPhone or Android app titled "Kay Warren," where you will find video messages from Kay, helpful resources, and daily challenges to courageously choose joy in every part of your life.

 Facebook Fan Page
Join Kay's Facebook community and "like" her fan page.

 Follow Kay on Twitter
Get encouragement and updates from Kay on Twitter: @KayWarren1

Visit www.KayWarren.com, email Kay@KayWarren.com, or call the office of Kay Warren at (949) 609-8552.

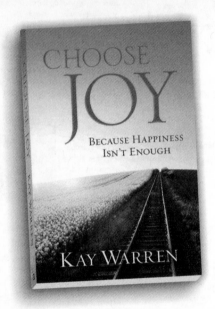